W9-BLY-798

COOL DISTANCE ASSISTANTS

Fun Science Projects to Propel Things

James Hopwood

ABDO
Publishing Company

TO ADULT HELPERS

You're invited to assist an up-and-coming scientist! And it will pay off in many ways. Your children can develop new skills, gain confidence, and do some interesting projects while learning about science. What's more, it's going to be a lot of fun!

These projects are designed to let children work independently as much as possible. Encourage them to do whatever they are able to do on their own. Also encourage them to try the variations when supplied and to keep a science journal. Encourage children to think like real scientists.

Before getting started, set some ground rules about using the materials and ingredients. Most important, adult supervision is a must whenever a child uses the stove, chemicals, or dry ice.

So put on your lab coats and stand by. Let your young scientists take the lead. Watch and learn. Praise their efforts. Enjoy the scientific adventure!

VISIT US AT WWW.ABDOPUBLISHING.COM

Published by ABDO Publishing Company, 8000 West 78th Street, Edina, Minnesota 55439. Copyright © 2008 by Abdo Consulting Group, Inc. International copyrights reserved in all countries. No part of this book may be reproduced in any form without written permission from the publisher. The Checkerboard Library™ is a trademark and logo of ABDO Publishing Company.

Printed in the United States.

Design and Production: Mighty Media, Inc.
Art Direction: Kelly Doudna
Photo Credits: Kelly Doudna, AbleStock, iStockphoto/Maartje van Caspel, JupiterImages Corporation, Photodisc, Shutterstock
Series Editor: Pam Price
Consultant: Scott Devens

The following manufacturers/names appearing in this book are trademarks: Back Trails, Crisco, Fiskars, Mettler, Ryobi, Scotch, Stanley, Wilson

Library of Congress Cataloging-in-Publication Data
Hopwood, James, 1964-
  Cool distance assistants : fun science projects to propel things / James Hopwood.
    p. cm. -- (Cool science)
  Includes index.
  ISBN-13: 978-1-59928-906-9
  1. Science projects--Juvenile literature. 2. Science--Experiments--Juvenile literature. I. Title.

  Q182.3.H67 2008
  507.8--dc22
                                2007015625

Contents

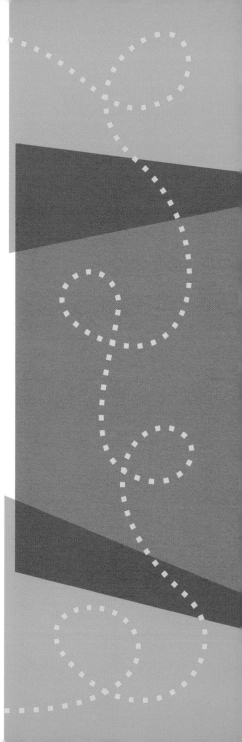

Science Is Cool

Welcome to the cool world of science! Before we get started, let's put on our thinking caps. What do the following things have in common?

- bubbles in soda pop
  - helium balloons that stay up in the air
    - sounds you hear through the headphones of your music player
      - a telescope that makes the faraway moon and stars appear closer
      - choosing your right or left eye to look through a camera viewfinder
  - your ability to balance on one foot

Did you guess that what they have in common is science? That's right, science! When you think of science, maybe you picture someone in a laboratory wearing a long white coat. Perhaps you imagine a scientist hunched over bubbling beakers and test tubes. But science is so much more. Let's take another look.

Soda pop doesn't develop bubbles until you open the container. That's because of a science called chemistry. Chemistry also explains why helium inside a balloon causes it to rise through the air.

You listen to your favorite song through the headphones attached to your music player. You look at the moon and stars through a telescope. Both activities are possible because of a science called physics. Did you know that eyeglasses improve your vision for the same reason telescopes work?

You tend to use the same eye each time you look through a camera viewfinder. You might find it challenging to balance on one foot. The science of biology helps explain why. Did you know it's related to the reason most people use only their left hand or right hand to write?

Broadly defined, science is the study of everything around us. Scientists use experiments and research to figure out how things work and relate to each other. The cool thing about science is that anyone can do it. You don't have to be a scientist in a laboratory to do science. You can do experiments with everyday things!

The Cool Science series introduces you to the world of science. Each book in this series will guide you through several simple experiments and projects with a common theme. The experiments use easy-to-find materials. Step-by-step instructions and photographs help guide your work.

The Scientific Method

Scientists have a special way of working. It is called the scientific method. The scientific method is a series of steps that a scientist follows when trying to learn something. Following the steps makes it more likely that the information you discover will be reliable.

The scientific method is described on the next page. Follow all of the steps. These steps will help you learn the best information possible. And then you can draw an accurate conclusion about what happened. You will even write notes in your own science journal, just like real scientists do!

EVEN COOLER!
Check out sections like this one throughout the book. Here you'll find instructions for variations on the project. It might be a suggestion for a different way to do the project. Or it might be a similar project that uses slightly different materials. Either way, it will make your science project even cooler!

1. Observe

Simply pay attention to something. This is called observing. A good way to prepare for the next step is to make up a what, why, or how question about what you observe. For example, let's say you observe that when you open a bottle of soda pop and pour it into a glass, it gets bubbly. Your question could be, How do bubbles get into soda?

2. Hypothesize

Think of a statement that could explain what you have observed. This statement is called a hypothesis. You might remember that you also saw bubbles in your milk when you blew into it with a straw. So your hypothesis might be, I think somebody used a straw to blow into the soda before the bottle was sealed.

3. Test

Test your hypothesis. You do this by conducting an experiment. To test your hypothesis about how bubbles get into soda, you might mix up a recipe, blow into the liquid with a straw, quickly close the container, and then open it back up.

4. Conclude

Draw a conclusion. When you do this, you tie together everything that happened in the previous steps. You report whether the result of the experiment was what you hypothesized. Perhaps there were no bubbles in your soda pop recipe when you reopened the container. You would conclude that blowing through a straw is not how fizz gets into liquids.

Write It Down

A large part of what makes science science is observation. You should observe what happens as you work through an experiment. Scientists observe everything and write notes about it in journals. You can keep a science journal too. All you need is a notebook and a pencil.

At the beginning of each activity in this book, there is a section called "Think Like a Scientist." It contains suggestions about what to record in your science journal. You can predict what you think will happen. You can write down what did happen. And you can draw a conclusion, especially if what really happened is different from what you predicted.

As you do experiments, record things in your journal. You will be working just like a real scientist!

THINK LIKE A SCIENTIST!
Look for a box like this one on the first page of each project. It will give you ideas about what to write in your science journal before, during, and after your experiments. There may be questions about the project. There may be a suggestion about how to look at the project in a different way. Your science journal is the place to keep track of everything!

EVEN COOLER!
You can record more than just words in your journal. You can sketch pictures and make charts. If you have a camera, you can even add photos to your journal!

Safe Science

Good scientists practice safe science. Here are some important things to remember.

- Check with an adult before you begin any project. Sometimes you'll need an adult to buy materials or help you handle them for a while. For some projects, an adult will need to help you the whole time. The instructions will say when an adult should assist you.

- Ask for help if you're unsure about how to do something.

- If you or someone else is hurt, tell an adult immediately.

- Read the list of things you'll need. Gather everything before you begin working on a project.

- Don't taste, eat, or drink any of the materials or the results unless the directions say that you can.

- Use protective gear. Scientists wear safety goggles to protect their eyes. They wear gloves to protect their hands from chemicals and possible burns. They wear aprons or lab coats to protect their clothing.

- Clean up when you are finished. That includes putting away materials and washing containers, work surfaces, and your hands.

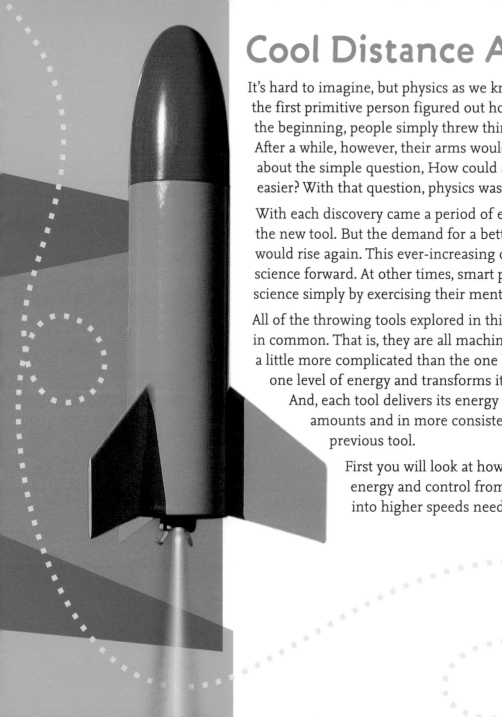

Cool Distance Assistants

It's hard to imagine, but physics as we know it today began when the first primitive person figured out how to throw a rock. In the beginning, people simply threw things with their hands. After a while, however, their arms would get tired. This brought about the simple question, How could a person throw things easier? With that question, physics was born.

With each discovery came a period of excitement about using the new tool. But the demand for a better way to toss things would rise again. This ever-increasing demand pulled the science forward. At other times, smart people advanced the science simply by exercising their mental muscles.

All of the throwing tools explored in this book have something in common. That is, they are all machines of sorts. Each one is a little more complicated than the one before. Each one takes one level of energy and transforms it to another level. And, each tool delivers its energy in potentially greater amounts and in more consistent ways than the previous tool.

First you will look at how to transform the energy and control from a person's muscles into higher speeds needed for throwing. Next

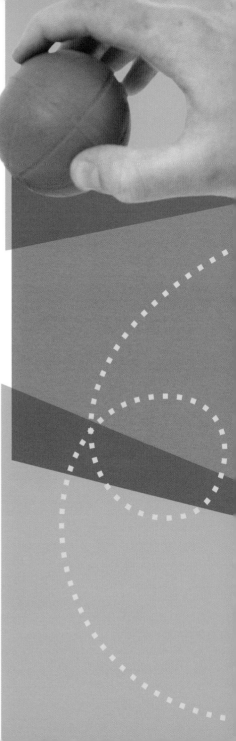

you will explore machines that store energy and release it in a controlled and constant way. These later devices have another big advantage. Their power is limited only by their size.

So retrace a little history, learn a little science, and build some cool backyard toys in the process. Yes, you can learn physics while examining how people play and compete in sports. You can even make a game of learning physics. So get your minds and muscles ready. It's time to get physical with physics!

Materials

You can probably find these supplies around the house.

marker

tennis balls

drill with bits

needle-nose pliers

wire hanger

field markers such as sticks, rocks, or crumpled paper

measuring tape

lightweight handle such as a garden stake or yardstick

plastic cooking spoon

duct tape

small rubber balls

object weighing 3 to 4 pounds (1.4 to 1.8 kg)

wooden yardstick

hot-glue gun

small saw

smooth paper clip

sturdy cardboard box

knife

plastic or foam golf balls

strong thread

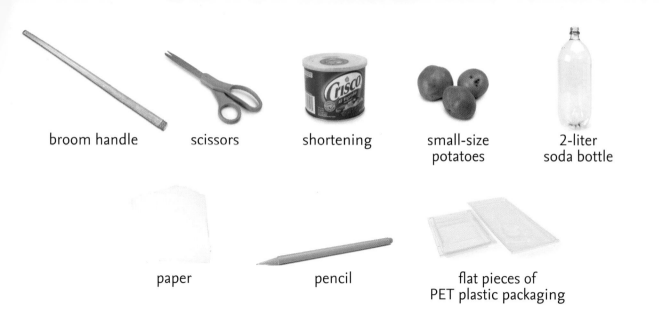

broom handle

scissors

shortening

small-size
potatoes

2-liter
soda bottle

paper

pencil

flat pieces of
PET plastic packaging

AT THE HARDWARE STORE
These supplies can be found at a hardware store.

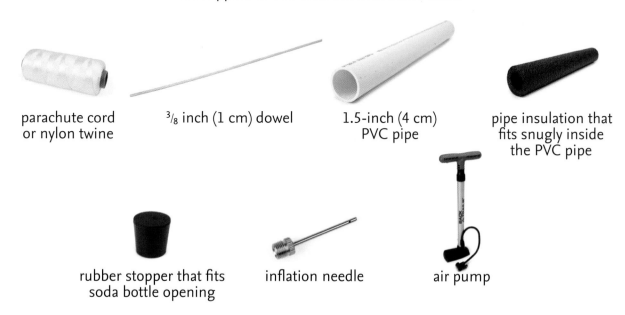

parachute cord
or nylon twine

$^3/_8$ inch (1 cm) dowel

1.5-inch (4 cm)
PVC pipe

pipe insulation that
fits snugly inside
the PVC pipe

rubber stopper that fits
soda bottle opening

inflation needle

air pump

Super Sling

TIME: ABOUT 45 MINUTES

To throw something farther, you need to throw it faster!

MATERIALS

marker

2 tennis balls

drill with a ¼-inch (6 mm) bit

needle-nose pliers

wire hanger

9 feet of parachute cord or nylon twine

field markers such as sticks, rocks, or crumpled paper

measuring tape

PHYSICS

THINK LIKE A SCIENTIST!

Write your observations about the experiment in your science journal. These questions will get you started.

1. What did you expect to happen?
2. What happened that you didn't expect?
3. Which is the best length of cord for slinging?
4. Would a stick work better for slinging than a string?
5. Would a dog like to chase this sling ball?

1. Mark two dots on opposite sides of one tennis ball. Have an adult helper drill a hole through one mark to pierce the surface of the ball.

2. On the opposite side, mark two more dots ¾-inch (2 cm) apart. The original dot should be centered between them. Drill a hole through each of the two new marks. Don't drill a hole at the original mark, though!

3. Use the pliers and the wire hanger to make a long hook that will fit through the holes.

4. Use the hook to pull one end of the cord in through the single hole and out one of the double holes. Use the hook again to loop the cord through the double holes. Tie the cord end securely to the exposed loop.

5. Take your new sling ball, the other tennis ball, and some field markers out to one end of a large, open field. Mark a starting point. Take a friend to help you mark where things land. That will make field-testing a lot easier.

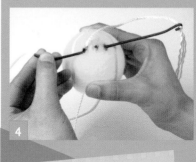

Science at Work

We still use the physics of the sling for **demolition**. A wrecking ball can bust a brick wall only when it moves fast enough. So a crane arm swings the wrecking ball on a cable, just like you swing the tennis ball. The crane moves a little at the top of the cable, and the ball swings a lot at the bottom. The ball doesn't move super fast, but it's so heavy that it builds a lot of energy as momentum. When that energy is applied to the bricks, they break.

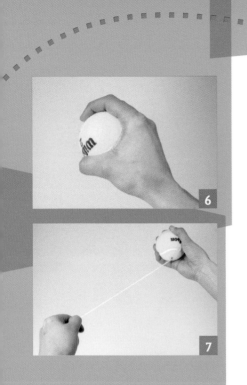

6 Throw the normal tennis ball as far as you can. Mark where it lands. If you think you can throw farther, give it another try.

7 Now grasp the sling cord about one foot from the ball. Swing the ball in a fast circle a few times and then release it. Mark where it lands. Throw the ball again, holding the cord at two feet out, then three feet out, and so on. Mark where each throw lands.

8 Note which throws went the farthest and which ones fell shortest.

9 Now that you know which cord length works best, tie a loop at that length and cut off the extra line. Using the loop you made, throw a few more times. See if you can beat your best throw.

The Science behind the Fun

When you use the sling to twirl the ball, you build up **velocity**. Increasing velocity is the secret to throwing farther. The energy held by the sling allows the ball to reach much faster speeds than if you simply throw the ball. Speed and mass work together to create momentum. Momentum is what keeps an object moving forward after you stop pushing it.

As you swing the ball on longer cords, the ball moves faster than your hand, gaining the momentum needed for longer throws. You may notice that the ball pulls harder against your hand as it moves faster. What you are feeling is an energy trade-off. The extra effort from your hand transforms into increased speed for the ball.

Funky Power Stick

TIME: ABOUT 10 MINUTES

A little **leverage** goes a long way to help fling things skyward.

PHYSICS

THINK LIKE A SCIENTIST!

Write your thoughts about the following in your science journal.

1. Did the stick help you throw farther?
2. Would redesigning the stick help you throw even farther? How would you redesign it and how would that help?
3. Would a scoop on a stick work with snowballs?

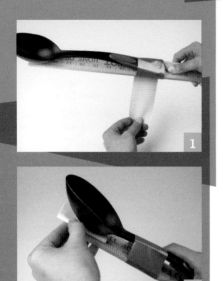

1 Tape the spoon securely to one end of the handle.

2 That's it! Now take your spoon on a stick, rubber balls, field markers, and tape measure to your test range. Take an assistant to help mark the landing points and find the rubber balls.

3 First mark your starting point. Now throw a few balls by hand to mark your unassisted throw distances.

4 Now take a few practice throws with the spoon. When you are ready, give a good, hard fling to see if you can pass your hand-thrown ball. Mark your results.

5 If the balls launch early and go too high, insert a larger paper wedge behind the spoon to increase its forward angle. If they launch too late and don't go high enough, use a smaller paper wedge to decrease the angle. Retest your device.

Science at Work

You might already be familiar with a throwing stick. Many call it a fishing pole. The rod's length, flexibility, and leverage allow an angler to launch a fishing lure far out over the water.

The Science behind the Fun

The stick extends the speed of your arm outward into a larger and faster arc, giving the ball greater momentum. If you snap your wrist, the ball will gain even more speed.

The stick has an advantage over the sling because it doesn't need constant energy to keep it rigid. That means you can throw when you are ready to. The stick also has a slight disadvantage. It doesn't allow you to build up speed by swinging it in circles.

Catapult in a Box

TIME: ABOUT 60 MINUTES

This **catapult** is actually a **trebuchet**. Remember that word if you want to sound smart. Remember why it works if you want to be smart.

FRONT

MATERIALS

3- to 4-pound (1.4 to 1.8 kg) counterweight such as a rock, splitting wedge, or hand weight

duct tape or packing tape

wooden yardstick

hot-glue gun

$^3/_8$ inch (1 cm) dowel or old arrow shaft

small saw

smooth paper clip

sturdy cardboard box about 12 × 12 × 20 inches (30 × 30 × 76 cm)

knife

plastic or foam golf ball

3 feet (0.9 m) of strong thread

adult helper

PHYSICS

THINK LIKE A SCIENTIST!

Answer these questions in your science journal.

1. How would a longer piece of thread affect the distance of the throw? What if the thread were shorter?

2. How would a heavier **counterweight** affect the distance of the throw?

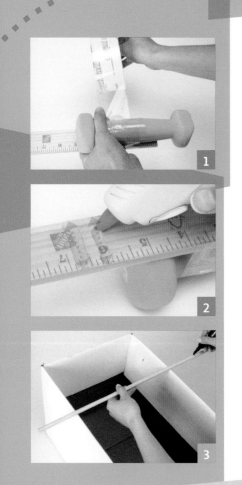

1 Tape the **counterweight** to the top of one end of the yardstick. Let it hang over the end of the stick a couple inches. Just be sure it is secure!

2 About 6.5 inches (16.5 cm) from the end with the weight, draw two parallel lines of hot glue across the bottom of the stick. They should be close together but not touching. Later the dowel will rest on this support notch. Make sure that the distance from the end of the counterweight to the glue notch is not longer than the height of the box.

3 The dowel should be about 6 inches (15.2 cm) longer than the width of the box. If needed, have an adult help you hold the dowel while you cut it with the saw. Center the dowel across the yardstick between the two glue lines and attach it with glue and tape.

Science at Work

People still design and build **trebuchets** and **catapults** to use in competitions. Most competitors today are physics and engineering students. Even with advanced materials, big math, and modern engineering, trebuchet design changed little until recently. The biggest design change came in the 1990s. It let the counterweight fall straight down on a track. The arm's pivot hinge was able to slide forward on a second track. This lets all the energy move in a single direction. Reportedly, this allowed a small machine to throw a golf ball 300 feet (91 m)!

4 Bend open the paper clip to expose the small loop. Place the paper clip on top of the free end of the yardstick so the end of the small loop overhangs by ⅜ inch (1 cm). Glue and tape it securely in place. This is your sling hook. That completes your **armature**.

5 If your box has lid flaps, fold them down inside the box. Tape them in place to add extra strength. Be sure the bottom is also securely taped.

6 Mark the front of your box. Measure from the tip of the counterweight to the center of the dowel. Add one inch to your measurement. Starting from the front of the box, measure back this distance along each side of the box. Mark these two spots. This measurement should be longer than the height of the box.

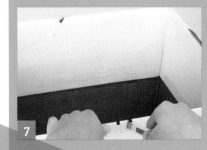

7 At each mark, have an adult help you cut a small notch in the edge of the box. The dowel will rest in these notches.

⭐💫

EVEN COOLER!

Try changing things up. Throw a rubber ball or change the length of your sling thread. Little changes can make big differences. Try launching the ball from the trebuchet arm alone. You may have to attach an egg carton cup to hold it in place for launching. You will see that the sling really adds speed to the throw.

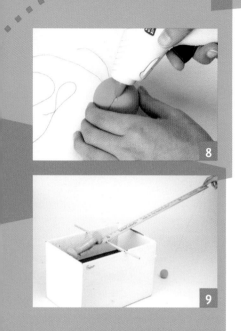

8 Tie one end of the thread to a ball. A knot held in place with a couple spots of glue works well for foam balls. Measure 15 inches (38 cm) of thread from the ball and tie a loop at that point. Trim off the extra thread.

9 Take your **trebuchet** outside to test it. Place the dowel in the notches with the **armature** on top. Press the long arm down to raise the weight. Place the loop in the thread over the sling hook and place the ball at the back of the box. When you're ready, release the arm. The machine will do the rest!

10 If necessary, fine-tune the trebuchet. If the ball flies too low, bend the paper clip back slightly to allow the thread to slip off a little earlier in the throw arc. If the ball goes too high, bend the clip a little forward to delay the ball release.

The Science behind the Fun

Swinging the raised weight down transfers its stored energy to the lever of the armature. Then the lever transfers the energy to the sling. Altogether, this gives the ball extra **acceleration** before it is released.

Watch the device work a few times and you will see that the **counterweight** doesn't move very fast or very far. The other end of the stick moves pretty fast compared with the weight. And the ball on the sling really moves! More impressive is that gravity essentially powers the whole thing. Notice how the ball lands in nearly the same place each time. Now that's precise!

Amazing Air Power

TIME: ABOUT 40 MINUTES

The secret to hurling something really far is to get as much high-speed energy behind it as possible. Here's how.

MATERIALS

¾-inch (2 cm) foam pipe insulation (should fit snugly inside the PVC pipe)

scissors

3-foot long (0.9 m) broom handle

hot-glue gun

duct tape

knife

2-foot (0.6 m) length of 1.5-inch (4 cm) PVC pipe

shortening

small-size potatoes

PHYSICS

THINK LIKE A SCIENTIST!
Write your thoughts about the following in your science journal.

1. Did the potato move faster than the plunger?

2. Does the tightness of the potato affect the power of the pop? How?

3. How far can you pop a potato? What could you try to pop your potato farther?

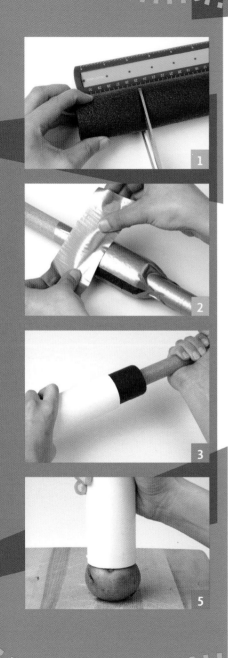

1. With the scissors, cut a two-inch (5 cm) length of pipe insulation. Glue it over one end of the broom handle. If needed, have an adult help you use a knife to whittle down the broom handle to fit inside the pipe insulation. This is your **piston** head.

2. Cut a second length of insulation about three inches (7.5 cm) long. Glue it to the broom handle 8 inches (20 cm) from the other end of the handle. Wrap this foam in duct tape to hold it firmly in place. This will protect your hand when you launch your potato.

3. Grease the inside of one end of the PVC pipe with shortening. Insert the piston head into the greased end of the pipe. Push the piston head all the way into the pipe. You now have a **compression** cylinder and a piston.

4. Grab a few potatoes and take everything outside. You're ready to test your device.

5. Place a potato on a firm surface. Pull back the piston to the end of the tube. Push the open end of the pipe straight down through the potato. This will create a potato plug on the discharge end of the PVC.

6. Hold the tube with one hand. With the other hand, grasp the piston behind the duct-taped foam ring. Point the pipe away from you. Push the piston through the pipe as fast as you can.

The Science behind the Fun

This device demonstrates compression and its sudden release. Pushing in the piston compresses the air between the moving plunger and the potato plug.

Eventually, the pressure builds and can overcome the **friction** between the potato and the tube. Then the potato will move out along the only available path. The energy of the compressed air pushes the potato, which **accelerates** until it escapes the tube. Then, the remaining compressed air explodes out as the plug leaves the tube. Pop goes the potato!

☆💫
EVEN COOLER!
Foam golf balls work great in place of potatoes. They do get a little squished, which makes them too lumpy to golf with. So be sure it's okay to use them.

Science at Work

Pressurized gas is used like a super spring in many industrial applications. It is a great way to capture and release energy at extremely fast or slow rates. Gas pressure can be gathered gradually through a pump or a boiler and released suddenly through a large **valve**. This is how they launch jets from the decks of ships. Or, gas pressure can be gathered suddenly and released slowly. This is how door closers close screen doors without slamming them.

Awesome Air & Water Rockets

TIME: ABOUT 65 MINUTES

So far you have **propelled** things away from your energy source. Now watch as an object is propelled by the energy stored within it.

MATERIALS

2-liter soda bottle

paper

pencil

marker

flat pieces of PET plastic packaging

heavy scissors

hot-glue gun

rubber stopper that fits the bottle opening

drill with a $\frac{1}{16}$-inch (1.6 mm) bit

inflation needle

air pump

PHYSICS

THINK LIKE A SCIENTIST!

Find a dry spot to sit after you've launched your rocket a few times. Write your thoughts about the following in your science journal.

1. Did the rocket work as well as you expected?
2. How did changing the amount of water affect the height the rocket reached?
3. If you were to do this again, what would you do differently?
4. Can you find better bottle rocket designs online?

1 Gather your materials. It may take a while to collect four pieces of PET large enough to make the tail fins. Watch what comes home in plastic packaging. The flat backside of heavy, formed plastic packaging is what you want.

2 Trace the shape of the bottle onto the paper. Draw a tail fin that will fit against the curved bottle top and provide a solid base. The top of the bottle will become the bottom of the rocket. Cut out the tail fin pattern and test it against the bottle to see if it fits tightly.

3 Trace the tail fin pattern onto the PET plastic at least four times. Carefully cut out the fins. If you have enough plastic to make a fifth fin, do it. The extra fin will help support the rocket when it is filled with water. The fins will also serve as the launch pad.

4 Mark the positions where you will mount the fins onto the bottle. Space them evenly around the bottle.

5 Hold each fin in place and mount it to the bottle with a thick bead of hot glue. The glue sticks to the plastic pretty well but doesn't fully bond, so use a lot. If the edges of the fins are sharp, wrap them in a thin strip of tape before you work with them.

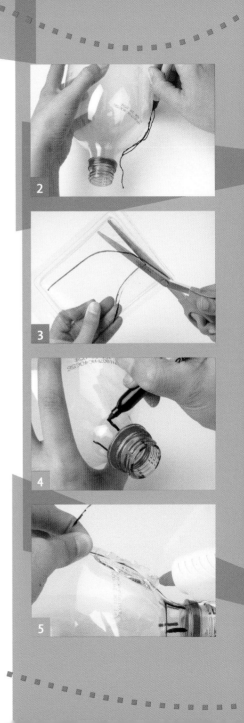

27

6 Now have an adult help you drill a small hole through the center of the rubber stopper. Push the inflation needle all the way through the hole. This needs to fit tightly, so if the hole is too big, seal the needle to the plug with a little glue. Be careful not to plug the needle with glue though.

7 Take the bottle, stopper, and pump outside for some field-testing. If you don't have a garden hose, bring a lot of water with you. By the way, this is the part where you get soaking wet!

8 Fill the bottle with water, stopping an inch (2.5 cm) from the top. Push the stopper in firmly. This is a test launch, so don't push the stopper in too hard.

9 Attach the pump to the needle threads and stand the rocket on its fins. If the stopper sticks out too far, you may need to dig a shallow hole.

Science at Work

We use rocketry to throw our **satellites** beyond the gravity of earth or even our solar system. Modern rocket scientists continue to look for more efficient ways to **propel** a rocket and its contents. They research new fuels that give more thrust per pound of fuel. They're even thinking about a nuclear rocket that shoots out a tiny stream of ions. It won't push as hard as a chemical fuel does, but it would provide a little bit of thrust for many years.

10 Pump up the rocket until the pressure inside the bottle pops the cork out. If the rocket flies a little bit, congratulations, you found a good pressure for your cork. If your rocket simply drains itself and falls over, push the plug in a bit more firmly next time.

11 Repeat this procedure, but put an inch (2.5 cm) less water in the bottle each time. Try to find the best balance of water and air space in your rocket to get the highest launch.

The Science behind the Fun

As you pump air into the rocket, the pressure inside the rocket increases. Compressed air is like a compressed spring that can store as much energy as its container can withstand. The more space the air has to fill, the more potential energy it can hold at any given pressure. The water in the rocket acts as a **counterweight**.

As the air pressure in the rocket shoots water downward, an equal amount of pressure is pushing upward, lifting the rocket higher. This is called thrust. As the water drains out, the rocket gets lighter. And, the air space increases as the water drains, so the pressure lowers. When the water is gone, the last bit of air pressure bursts out but provides very little thrust.

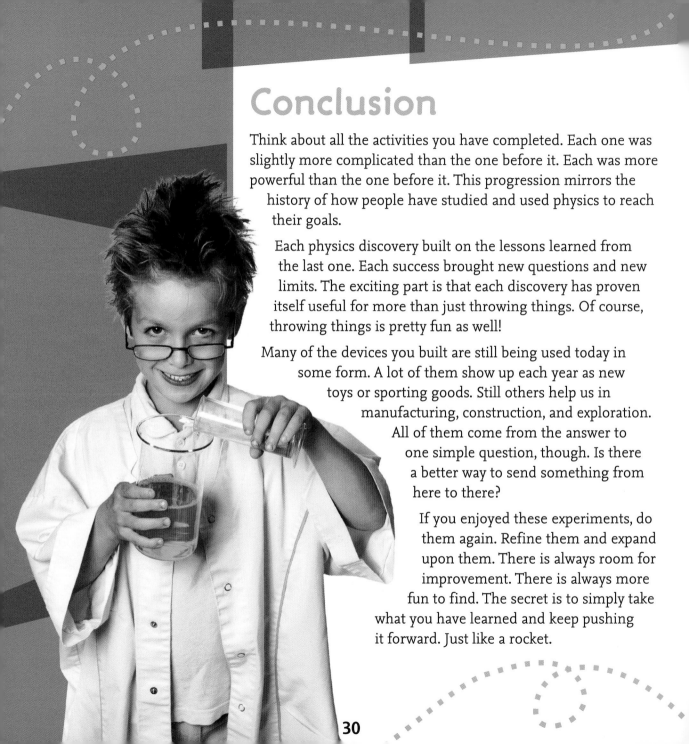

Conclusion

Think about all the activities you have completed. Each one was slightly more complicated than the one before it. Each was more powerful than the one before it. This progression mirrors the history of how people have studied and used physics to reach their goals.

Each physics discovery built on the lessons learned from the last one. Each success brought new questions and new limits. The exciting part is that each discovery has proven itself useful for more than just throwing things. Of course, throwing things is pretty fun as well!

Many of the devices you built are still being used today in some form. A lot of them show up each year as new toys or sporting goods. Still others help us in manufacturing, construction, and exploration. All of them come from the answer to one simple question, though. Is there a better way to send something from here to there?

If you enjoyed these experiments, do them again. Refine them and expand upon them. There is always room for improvement. There is always more fun to find. The secret is to simply take what you have learned and keep pushing it forward. Just like a rocket.

Glossary

acceleration – an increase in velocity.

armature – in a trebuchet, the arm that transfers energy from the counterweight to the item being launched.

catapult – an ancient device for launching things such as stones or arrows. Today, the word *catapult* more often refers to the type of device used to launch planes from ship decks.

compression – the act of pressing something together to reduce its size, quantity, or volume.

counterweight – an equal weight or force that balances another weight.

demolition – the act of tearing down or destroying something.

friction – the force that resists motion between two objects that are touching.

leverage – the force or power gained by using a lever.

piston – a mechanical device that moves inside a cylinder to create compression.

propel – to push or move forward.

satellite – a manufactured object launched to orbit the earth or other planet, moon, or star.

trebuchet – a medieval weapon used to hurl heavy rocks.

valve – a mechanical device that controls the flow of gas, liquids, or other materials through a pipe, duct, or other passageway.

velocity – the rate of change of the speed and direction of a moving object.

WEB SITES

To learn more about leverage and throwing things, visit ABDO Publishing Company on the World Wide Web at **www.abdopublishing.com.** Web sites about leverage and throwing things are featured on our Book Links page. These links are routinely monitored and updated to provide the most current information available.

Index